RAILWAY ARCHITECTURE

Bill Fawcett

Published in Great Britain in 2015 by Shire Publications Ltd, PO Box 883, Oxford, OX1 9PL, UK.

PO Box 3985, New York, NY 10185-3985, USA.

E-mail: shire@shirebooks.co.uk
www.shirebooks.co.uk

A CIP catalogue record for this book is available from the British Library.

Shire Library no. 806.   ISBN-13: 978 0 74781 445 0
PDF e-book ISBN: 978 1 78442 048 2
ePub ISBN: 978 1 78442 047 5

Bill Fawcett has asserted his right under the Copyright, Designs and Patents Act, 1988, to be identified as the author of this book.

Typeset in Garamond Pro and Gill Sans.

Printed in China through Worldprint Ltd.

15 16 17 18 19   10 9 8 7 6 5 4 3 2 1

COVER IMAGE
Cover design and photography by Peter Ashley. Front cover: Oakham station, Rutland. Back cover: British Railways totem sign, Heckington station, Lincolnshire.

TITLE PAGE IMAGE
Wemyss Bay station, Renfrewshire (1903), was the Caledonian Railway's showpiece railhead for local commuters and its ferry service to the Isle of Bute.

CONTENTS PAGE IMAGE
William Hamlyn's 1938 concourse at Leeds City station depicted in a British Railways' carriage print.

ACKNOWLEDGMENTS
I should like to thank the following people and organisations for allowing me to use images:

Alamy, page 17 (bottom); Tyne & Wear Museums & Archives/The Bridgeman Art Library, page 36; David Flett, page 19 (bottom); Science & Society Picture Library, pages 3 and 10 (top); Wikicommons, page 6 (top); Wikicommons/Tom Heyes, page 50 (top left); David Wilson, page 21 (top); Piotr Wlodarczyk, page 41. All other illustrations are by the author or from his collection.

I should also like to acknowledge the many friends who, over the years, have contributed to my knowledge and understanding of railway history and architecture.

Shire Publications is supporting the Woodland Trust, the UK's leading woodland conservation charity, by funding the dedication of trees.

CONTENTS

GETTING STARTED

Britain's railway buildings evoke the country's rise as the world's first great industrial power while also reflecting the architectural currents of their time. Causey Arch in County Durham (1727) reminds us that railways derived from wooden-railed, horse-drawn wagonways, generally carrying coal and stone, but between 1790 and 1830 they evolved into major public carriers using iron rails and steam locomotives, and requiring specialised buildings.

The Stockton & Darlington Railway (September 1825) demonstrates this. At first its locomotives hauled only coal and mineral trains while contractors employed horses for other goods and passengers. Operational buildings were confined to toll houses, workshops, and engine houses both for locomotives and for the winding engines providing rope haulage over the Brusselton and Etherley Ridges. After a year, the goods and passenger traffic justified the company building a warehouse at Darlington, along with inns for waiting passengers, at Stockton, Darlington and Heighington. The last included an agent's office and is the oldest surviving building at any operational station, though no longer used by the railway. Only a fragment remains of the Brusselton incline engine house but the Cromford & High Peak Railway (now a country trail) in Derbyshire retains one at Middleton Top (1830), as well as a transhipment warehouse (1832) at Whaley Bridge. Darlington's North Road Museum conserves the Stockton & Darlington's 1833 goods station and 1842 passenger station.

Middleton Top engine house, Derbyshire, was preserved following closure in 1963 and retains the two-cylinder beam engine supplied in 1829, albeit with many parts renewed. Wagons were hauled up and down the incline on an endless wire rope.

Causey Arch near Stanley, County Durham, was built in 1727 for the Tanfield wagonway. Its 32-metre span, then the largest stone arch in Britain, emphasises the profitability of some early wagonways.

Formal station buildings originated with the Liverpool & Manchester Railway (1830), which provided these at its termini though not, for some years, at wayside stops. Its Manchester station survives as a museum. A low brick viaduct sandwiched between this and the goods warehouse bore trains at first-floor level. First- and second-class passengers were segregated throughout, with separate entrances, booking halls

Stockton Toll House, seen around 1970 before the tracks were taken up, was one of three designed by John Carter in classic turnpike fashion. Each had a wagon-weighing machine so that the appropriate toll could be calculated.

and stairs up to the waiting rooms and platform. Cross-walls divided the warehouse into compartments served by branch tracks at right angles to the running line, wagons being swung into these on hand-operated turnplates.

Whaley Bridge, Derbyshire. Integrated transport: the warehouse provided shelter for transhipment between a branch of the Peak Forest Canal and flanking railway tracks that entered through the two big arches.

Early passenger carriages required covered storage, so the Manchester station was quickly extended to provide a carriage shed reached via turnplates, with retail units below; the resulting street frontage resembles a row of houses. The Liverpool terminus has vanished but had a platform canopy, soon augmented by a wooden carriage shed over the main tracks, forming a prototype for the trainsheds that came to epitomise major stations.

Newtyle station (1831–2), formerly served by a railway from Dundee, is another early survivor – a goods shed with passenger platform at one end. The oldest remaining passenger trainshed is at Selby (1834), terminus of a line from Leeds and transfer point for river steamers to Hull; this was roofed in three spans, with the passenger station in the middle and goods either side. The transfer of passengers to

Manchester Liverpool Road terminus, now the Museum of Science and Industry; on the left is the passenger station, with the carriage shed at this end; the goods warehouse is on the right.

STATION BUILDING 3

The Euston entrance screen (Philip Hardwick). The portico led into a courtyard with the station on the right and a vacant plot opposite, originally intended for the Bristol line (Great Western) terminus. The station soon expanded into all this space.

new premises (1841) ensured its survival as a goods station and now private warehousing.

Rich, proud Liverpool brought the next progression in passenger termini. In 1836 the station moved to Lime Street, opposite the 'Plateau', earmarked as a civic forum. For the first time a station would become a townscape feature, so the council funded a neo-classical screen to platforms and trainshed. There were two platforms: one for departures, flanked by waiting rooms and offices, and one for arrivals, flanked by a cab road. This set the pattern for termini for years to come.

Hard on Liverpool's heels came London's Euston station (1837–8, demolished), serving Robert Stephenson's Birmingham line, one of the first trunk railways. It featured a frontal screen with a giant Doric portal, but equally significant was the two-span trainshed, which pioneered the railway use of a light wrought-iron truss, based on developments in workshop and warehouse roofs. 'Euston trusses' became widely popular, and their early character can still be appreciated in Scarborough station (1845).

Northumberland has the oldest surviving engine shed: Greenhead (1836), a long narrow building, later used for road vehicles. This form remained commonplace but others developed alongside, notably the 'roundhouse', which held engines stabled on spur roads radiating from a turntable. Few roundhouses remain in Britain, and none are in railway use, but they include an early example at Derby (1840) by Stephenson and his architect, Francis Thompson. Along with contemporaneous workshops and offices, it has been conserved under the name 'Pride Park'. Chalk Farm in London retains the 1847 roundhouse that served Euston, and is now a well-known arts venue, while Leeds (Holbeck) has two: a stylish twenty-two-road shed (1850) with an open turntable encircled by a stone arcade, and a half roundhouse of 1864. The latter form was unusual in Britain but common in Germany, where a number remain in operation.

The railways' visual impact in the landscape was modest at first and William Jessop's 1811 viaduct at Laigh Milton, Ayrshire, on the Kilmarnock & Troon Railway had few rivals for almost two decades. Then much larger masonry bridges began to proliferate but their technology was still that of

The Euston-style trainshed at Scarborough (George Townsend Andrews, 1845). The columns sit on stone blocks that have been exposed by lowering the tracks to obtain higher platforms.

York Roundhouse no. 2 (demolished) with a typical raised roof (1889) above the central turntable. It had sixteen roads, one occupied by the entrance. The locomotive is a short-lived Great Eastern Railway express design of 1898.

Primrose Hill Tunnel, London: east portal (1837). The artist has introduced a surveyor, right, taking a sighting on to the tall pole, to emphasise the engineering involved. A second tunnel, with matching entrance, was built alongside in 1879.

Ballochmyle Viaduct, Ayrshire (John Miller, 1848). The 55.4-metre central arch is the largest masonry span of any British railway bridge.

Smeaton and Telford, even in the great span at Ballochmyle (1848) on the line from Dumfries to Glasgow. A notable early viaduct is Balcombe, West Sussex (1841), whose thirty-seven graceful arches bear a balustrade framed by arched loggias. This was a calculated embellishment, whereas Berwick-upon-Tweed's even larger Royal Border Bridge (1850) is a simple design made notable by its estuarine setting. Tunnel portals lent themselves to symbolic architectural treatment, the grandest early example being Primrose Hill, where Stephenson's Birmingham railway bursts into London through a display conjured up by his secretary, W. H. Budden.

A RAPID ADVANCE: 1840–59

THREE PIONEERING RAILWAY engineers died in successive years: Robert Stephenson and Isambard Brunel in 1859; Joseph Locke in 1860. By then, most of the present network had been completed, hastened by the 1840s' 'Railway Mania' investment boom that encouraged promoters, conscious of their image, to be liberal about buildings. The results frequently display a vitality and variety that became less common later on.

In this period iron bridges extended into novel forms, with three attracting particular interest. Stephenson's High Level Bridge at Newcastle upon Tyne (1849) developed existing tied-arch concepts to provide a double-decker, with railway tracks borne above a road deck. His Britannia Bridge over the Menai Strait (1850) required main spans of 140 metres, an unprecedented length save for suspension bridges, so was conceived as a wrought-iron box girder with the railway inside. Steel arches were substituted after fire damage in 1970 but Conwy Bridge (1849) on the same route retains its tubes. A decade later, Brunel faced the same challenge at Saltash, where the railway is carried into Cornwall by two spans of 139 metres, hung by rigid struts from arched wrought-iron tubes.

Both men favoured one-sided layouts for important through stations but they meant different things. Stephenson's ideal, exemplified by Chester (1848), comprised one long through platform, with a central crossover enabling it to house two trains simultaneously, together with terminal bays at each end. One suite of waiting and refreshment rooms sufficed for all passengers and they had no need to cross the tracks. His favourite architect, Francis Thompson, responded with Chester's immensely long but boldly articulated façade. Brunel's scheme is typified by Taunton, which had separate, self-contained stations for each direction, both on the same side of the line. This needless duplication of facilities was abandoned in later rebuilding but his 1842 office range survives.

Brunel's innovations at his Bristol terminus (1840) were more worthwhile. The tracks were elevated, with booking hall and arrival arcade tucked beneath the two platforms, housed in a trainshed whose elegant mock hammerbeam roof maintained the Tudor image of the company offices. These were set across the head of the station to create an impressive street frontage, anticipating how hotels would exploit and emphasise the urban presence of later termini. Nowadays the showpiece is the arched wrought-iron shed added for through traffic (Francis Fox, 1878); since 1965 all trains have

Newcastle's High Level Bridge has an architectural quality deriving from its enclosed form, with the railway borne on cast-iron arches, and a roadway hanging from them.

been handled there and at further platforms of 1935. Aspects of Bristol, including columns inconveniently fringing the platform edge, were echoed in numerous 'Brunel barns', the timber trainsheds that accompanied wooden office buildings at too many of his town stations. These could be elegant, such as Merthyr Tydfil (1853), with its scissors truss given an arched soffit by curving brackets, but the only survivors are the utilitarian Frome, Somerset (1850), and the posthumous Kingswear, Devon (1864), both by assistants.

Station-masters lived on the job so the role model for early wayside stations was the picturesque entrance lodge to a country estate. The 1835 station building at Hexham, Northumberland, is the oldest still in use: originating as a four-room cottage with a porch housing the public room, but now embraced by the offices and platform roof soon required at a bustling country town. Along with Sleaford, Lincolnshire (1857), it is a classic example of ad-hoc growth to cope with the rapid rise in business and in passenger expectations.

Brunel opted to keep house and station apart, enabling him to develop standard designs with a broad cantilevered awning

Brunel's Bristol Temple Meads with a train newly arrived from London behind the locomotive *Arrow*. The traverser, in the foreground, was used to move carriages sideways between the departure line, on the left, and the two sidings alongside.

Culham,
Oxfordshire.
The cast-iron
brackets have
been added
to strengthen
the roof, while
the frilly wooden
valancing, on
the left, is also
a later feature.

wrapped round the offices to shelter both platform and roadside. Culham (1844), on the Great Western Railway's Oxford line, is the last survivor of his original Tudor design, though some derived from this exist, notably Crediton, Devon (1856). More examples remain of an Italianate cousin with offices and awning under a prominent hipped roof. The Duke of Wellington's local station, Mortimer, Berkshire (1848), has this and a matching waiting shed on the second platform, both in brick. Charlbury, Oxfordshire (1853), has the timber version, and there is a more ornate example at Torre, Devon (1848).

Some architects saw platform roofs as visual nuisances, compromising their designs, but John Livock had no such qualms. He worked extensively for the London & Birmingham and associated railways, though little remains. For their Peterborough branch (1845) he provided Tudor/Jacobean stations with prominent flat awnings cantilevered out on wooden brackets. Wansford is the best survivor, accompanied by a matching terrace of houses, but the awning has long gone; likewise at Atherstone, Warwickshire (1847), a fine essay in manorial Tudor. The most extensive platform roofs of the period are found on the main line linking the Firths of Forth and Tay, where stations in a hybrid Tudor/Italian manner have flat awnings on slender cast-iron columns.

The largest is Cupar (1847), its frontage conceived as three linked pavilions; adjoining is a gutsy overbridge with Tudor touches. This pavilion approach achieved an impressively broad show-front by incorporating houses at each end, and was also adopted for Stowmarket, Suffolk (1846), whose parish authorities helped finance an ensemble matching their vision for the town.

Benjamin Green's suave Jacobethan designs for the main line from Newcastle to Berwick (1847) employed discreet awnings carefully integrated into the façade, still extant at Chathill and Acklington, along with original waiting sheds on the second platform. Acklington also retains its goods shed (now a house) in matching style. A Gothic alternative, rare at this date, is provided by G. T. Andrews's Thorp Arch, West Yorkshire (1847), where a large platform verandah is provided by sweeping the office roof down on to chunky timber columns.

It was left to Sancton Wood and Francis Thompson to highlight the formal potential of platform and entrance awnings. Wood probably originated the concept at Audley End, Essex (1845), where an Italianate block with roof sunk behind the parapet is flanked by low wings with screen

Oundle, Northampton-shire. John Livock's Peterborough branch station survives as a house but without the characteristic awning seen in this early twentieth-century view, let alone any trains.

Stowmarket, by Ipswich architect Frederick Barnes, is an essay in the late sixteenth-century manner. Nearby Needham Market is a smaller and more tightly massed design, even more evocative of the Elizabethan age.

walls projecting to frame a flat canopy. It came to maturity in Thompson's work for the Chester & Holyhead Railway, notably Holywell, Flintshire (1848), whose walls are capped to create the illusion of a shallow, Roman-tiled roof. The awnings have gone but the dainty pavilions that embraced the platform roof remain.

Holywell may have influenced the careful massing of William Tress's Italianate Rye station, East Sussex (1851), with its arched portico neatly tucked into the façade, while at Battle (1852) this feature reappears on the platform frontage of a handsome Gothic design – his acknowledgement to the town's former abbey. Similar feelings governed G .T. Andrews's response to a picturesque setting at Richmond, North Yorkshire (1847), with a tightly knit Gothic station embracing a cloistral portico and steeply gabled trainshed.

Before platform roofing properly evolved, country-town and junction stations often warranted small trainsheds. Most have been lost, but there are six complete survivors by Andrews, of which three in Yorkshire still handle trains: Scarborough (1845), Filey (1847) and Pickering (1847, reinstated 2011). Chard, Somerset (1866), retains the last small shed by Francis Fox, Brunel's successor at the Bristol & Exeter Railway; trains ceased in 1962 but it survives in industrial use. The bracing winds of Caithness have ensured the retention of trainsheds at Wick and Thurso (1874), sturdy jobs with old-fashioned timber roofs. These contrast with the sophisticated iron Polonceau trusses (the norm for French stations) of Edinburgh's first terminus, Haymarket (1842), transferred in preservation to Bo'ness on the Forth.

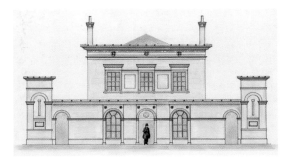

Windsor's Riverside station (1851) is by Sir William Tite, who routinely designed the buildings on Locke's railways. Its Tudor Revival building heads a long trainshed that curves down to the former royal waiting rooms. The booking hall is symbolised by an oriel-windowed gable, which derives from his earlier station at Penrith, Cumbria (1846). Tite's most ambitious essays in this genre are Carlisle (1847) and Perth (1848) but the trainsheds there have been replaced.

Holywell in its original form; it is now a private house, minus awnings but otherwise restored. Nearby Flint is still a busy station, retaining its original platform and entrance roofs but displaying a more picturesque, less formal character.

Rye, with its end bays framing the portico and the higher block behind. The platform awning, dating from 1895, is not entirely sympathetic. A mildly Italianate one-storey gatekeeper's cottage by Tress stands at the nearby road crossing.

Carlisle: Tite's 1847 office range now fronts an impressively large and light trainshed of 1881, whose gables can be seen poking up behind.

A station sited near the town centre might compromise historic views, as at Conwy and Shrewsbury, where lines run alongside the castle walls. Thomas Penson responded at Shrewsbury (1849) with a lavish collegiate-Tudor display, rendered more effective by its underpinning with another storey in 1903. His wayside stations (1846–8) between Chester and Shrewsbury are of equal quality: Whittington is a particularly fine Tudor example, accompanied by a smaller but equally well-detailed house for the crossing keeper, while Gobowen has a Florentine villa, complete with campanile. Bells were often used to signal train departures and gave Sancton Wood the excuse for a belfry at his Stamford station (1848), a feature reprised with gusto at Portarlington, Ireland (1851).

Stations as the focus of a planned townscape are rare in Britain but Huddersfield was being remodelled when the railway arrived (1847), so the two companies involved

Shrewsbury's canopy eaves mark the original ground level, which sloped down to the far end, where Penson added the three-storey wing in 1855. The rest of the building was dug beneath and underpinned for today's ground floor in 1903.

Huddersfield: the nearer portico was the entrance to a booking office, marked by company heraldry above the parapet. The trainshed, of no particular distinction, was replaced by the present, larger one in 1886.

engaged J. P. Pritchett, active locally, for a neo-classical design forming a superb backdrop to a new square. Harmony was achieved by putting refreshment rooms behind the main portico and booking offices at the extremities, an arrangement later reversed. The only pure classical design of comparable quality is Monkwearmouth, Sunderland (1848), again by a local man: Thomas Moore.

Stoke-on-Trent has an entire square created by the North Staffordshire Railway, with Henry Hunt's richly Jacobean station (1848) facing a hotel and housing for senior officers. Its cousin is Hunt's triangular block within the junction at Stone. Stoke housed the head office and these could yield ambitious stations in unlikely places. The classic example is the Cambrian Railways Company, formed by amalgamation (1864) and acquiring four surprisingly large stations. Oswestry and

Ellesmere, Shropshire (1863), were headquarters while Llanidloes, Powys (1862), may have been conceived thus. Welshpool, Powys (1864), was not, yet is the most striking: a Franco-Tudor essay by Thomas Penson. The Oswestry works (1866 onwards) closed in 1967 but, adapted for commercial use, still gives a good impression of a railway's main workshops.

Increasing sophistication in large stations emerges with Cambridge (1845) and Bury St Edmunds, Suffolk (1847). Bury's platforms are at first-floor level, where Sancton Wood provided a trainshed framed by baroque turrets, beyond which a screen wall features a giant arcade containing the entrance. Wood was superseded as architect for Cambridge by Thompson, who may have adopted some of his ideas. The outcome broke new ground, with a tall arcaded carriage porch forming the entire frontage; it wrapped round the ends to provide formal entries for the tracks into the trainshed.

Bury St Edmunds continues to the left as a Tudor range with waiting rooms upstairs and the station house below. Sancton Wood used similar baroque turrets to frame his Dublin (Heuston) station of 1848.

The offices were completely screened by the portico, allowing them to be treated in a less formal way if function so dictated.

This idea was taken further in the original scheme for Newcastle upon Tyne (1850) by the leading local architect, John Dobson. His 1846 design had a baroque liveliness, with the frontage formed by a pedestrian arcade punctuated by a giant carriage porch, articulated with columns and statuary. Work began, but the economic downturn afflicting all railways by 1849 led to the scheme being simplified; the arcade was omitted, and the portico was delayed until 1863. Nonetheless, the final result marked a new grandeur in railway design while Dobson's trainshed ushered in the era of multiple-span arched roofs.

Newcastle Central station is a work of tremendous panache, almost anticipating the American *Beaux Arts* designs at the end of the century. It and François Dusqueney's Paris Gare de l'Est (1850) are the finest railway buildings of their time.

MATURITY IN SMALL TO MEDIUM BUILDINGS

By 1860 station facilities had matured into a form that would endure for the next hundred years. A basic station might have just a booking hall, doubling as waiting room, accompanied by a booking office and toilets. Third-class passengers originally were expected to wait on the platform but, with 'respectable' travellers increasingly switching from second to third, some stations acquired a general room supplemented by first and ladies' waiting rooms. Larger stations might have separate rooms for every class and gender, plus segregated refreshment rooms, while the burgeoning traffic in parcels by passenger train often required further office space.

Although more than a hundred undertakings made up the railways, about thirty companies were significant players. The top four, by capital and income, were the LNWR (London & North Western), Great Western, Midland, and North Eastern, which employed their own architects and engineers and only occasionally turned to private practitioners. With this went increasing standardisation of designs, seen at its most extreme on the LNWR, which manufactured timber building modules for use throughout the system. These are no longer common, but a classic example exists at Prestatyn, Denbighshire (1897).

For wayside stations a common choice was the cottage style, with cross gables framing a platform recess covered by either the main roof or a glazed awning, an arrangement both

Nottingham (Midland Railway, 1904) makes extensive use of terracotta, favoured over stone because it could be kept clean in a smoky atmosphere; good examples of architectural faience also exist in the refreshment rooms down on the platforms.

Prestatyn is a well-restored example of LNWR modular wooden buildings with their distinctive tripartite windows. The platform has been rebuilt with the precast concrete components commonly used since the 1930s.

picturesque and practical. Best-known are those on the Settle & Carlisle route (John Sanders, 1876), which are among the few survivors from the Midland Railway's once extensive range. The Great Central Railway used a larger version, typified by Dinting, Derbyshire (1884), and gave Mexborough, South Yorkshire (1871), a superior one featuring a stone arcade on iron columns.

A stretched cottage plan became characteristic of the Highland Railway. Tain, Ross-shire (1864), is an early instance

Mexborough. A stone arcade on cast-iron columns featured also at the North Eastern's Rowley station (William Peachey, 1873, with handsome barley-twist columns), which has been re-erected at Beamish Museum (County Durham).

but examples became common only from 1885 as replacement buildings, usually with refined Tudor detailing and often with stepped gables; Pitlochry, Perthshire, and Nairn (1885) are particularly good examples. An Italianate version of the cottage plan is seen at the South Eastern Railway's North Camp, Aldershot (about 1860), a polychrome brick pavilion that, toned down, became the basis for a standard design. A Midland equivalent is found at Ilkley, West Yorkshire (1865), with stone arches screening the recess.

The Great Western employed standardised designs from the outset, but the pleasing Italianate buildings of 1872 at Taplow, Buckinghamshire (enlarged 1884), appeared just as a new rigour was setting in. The new style featured segmental openings with prominent stone lintels spanning two-light windows, as at Moreton-in-Marsh, Gloucestershire (1873), where the harsh brickwork looks particularly inappropriate. Some were tricked out with 'Frenchy' pavilion roofs and iron cresting to enliven them, and a few could be genuinely good.

An eastbound freight at Nairn in 1994. The other platform has a large, elegant timber waiting-room range though by far the most ambitious of the Highland Railway's wooden stations is at the popular resort of Aviemore (1892).

Horton-in-Ribblesdale typifies the Midland's Settle & Carlisle line. Note the portable steps, traditionally used at stations with low platforms.

At Torquay, Devon (1878), standard building blocks are transformed by the use of local stone and clever integration of the footbridge and its towers. The platform awnings there and at Wrexham (1881) typify the GWR's best, with slender, widely spaced columns supporting a pitched roof with a raised skylight close to the wall. In the 1890s the GWR became one of the earliest companies to dispense with cast-iron columns and to fabricate roofs entirely using rolled-steel sections, as seen at Newbury, Berkshire (1910), alongside a fashion for hefty lintels in stylised Tudor – a period trademark.

One of the glories of British railway architecture is the extensive use of glazed ridge-and-furrow roofs, a type seldom found abroad. For this we must thank Sir Joseph Paxton, who developed them for horticulture. He then used them for his Crystal Palace, whose contractors, Fox & Henderson, employed them the same year, 1851, at Oxford's Rewley Road station, later remodelled and now translated to Quainton Road, Buckinghamshire.

They became synonymous with the Midland, which introduced them on its main line from Leicester to Hitchin (1857), engineered by Charles Liddell, whose staff designer, Charles Driver, gave the stations a Gothic flavour, albeit with round-arched windows featuring diamond-pattern panes. The smaller stations, typified by Glendon & Rushton, Northamptonshire, included a small cross-gabled waiting shed. Larger ones employed fully glazed ridge-and-furrow

Thomas Penson's Wrexham station was replaced in 1881 by this building, whose platform roof is identical to those at Torquay. The far platform structures and footbridge date from around 1912.

Torquay station was rebuilt in local limestone, with the iron-crested pavilion roof stepping gracefully up into the footbridge tower. Tiverton, built shortly afterwards (1885), was similar but with gabled roofs; it has been demolished.

awnings. Wellingborough survives complete, its polychrome brickwork and graceful cast-iron brackets hinting at the riches Driver would later provide for London's Abbey Mills pumping station. The goods shed is in matching style.

The open gables seen in early roofs were generally superseded by hipped ends to give a crisp edge, as in the Furness Railway's handsome station at Grange-over-Sands, Cumbria (1872), fruit of their prolonged patronage of the Lancaster architect Edward Paley. However, the Great Eastern made a feature of the sawtooth profile, accentuated by deep timber valancing,

Wellingborough's verandah originally had filigree ironwork in the open gable ends. A comparable roof survives at Kettering, though its accompanying building has been replaced.

The roof at Grange-over-Sands employs standard rolled sections perched above spandrel panels of unusual delicacy. The coming of the railway established Grange as a genteel resort.

for the shallow, unglazed roofs which lend distinction to many east London stations; notable examples are Bruce Grove and Hackney Downs, the latter somewhat altered but featuring a variety of interesting ironwork.

In Scotland, Glasgow & South Western stations, notably Dumfries, followed the Midland roofing pattern while the North British opted for a heavier design with larger bays and only partial glazing, as at Coatbridge (Sunnyside), Lanarkshire (1886). The North Eastern also went for large bays but employed excellent decorative ironwork. Their most flamboyant example is Tynemouth, Tyne and Wear (1883). Built to serve holiday as well as local traffic, it represents the company's standard design of that time in its fully glazed form, with the cast-iron detail augmented by wrought-iron filigree work.

The most exotic platform ironwork must be that at Great Malvern, Worcestershire, where Edmund Elmslie's vigorous Gothic station (1862) is accompanied by wrought-iron column capitals representing a variety of local plants. Thirty years later, changing tastes and the adoption of steel joists produced the much simpler ridge-and-furrow roof at the Midland's Bingley station, West Yorkshire – a compact design exploiting the sloping site to place a cottage-style entrance building at the side, leading straight into the footbridge.

Compact stations, requiring minimal land, would result from placing the entrance building on a bridge. This became common in London, Denmark Hill (1865) being a striking example, with a booking hall clasped between low wings framing a flat awning with

Great Malvern's foliage capitals were created by William Forsyth, best-known locally as a very able carver in wood and stone.

rich cast-iron brackets and balustrade. The detail is a classic High Victorian synthesis from varied sources; the architect was Charles Driver, whose Battersea Park (1867) reverses the situation: with the railway high above the street, he exploited the space to create a lofty booking hall in the angle of two lines.

The Lancashire & Yorkshire frequently used bridge frontages: generally dull affairs such as the big barn at Bolton, Greater Manchester (1904). That has gone but its platforms are still graced by good examples of the company's awnings and buildings. The Midland did things better, as at Leicester and Nottingham, both featuring an enclosed, glass-roofed cab-stand as their frontage. Leicester (1895) is by Charles Trubshaw, company architect, with a showy screen wall featuring much terracotta. Nottingham (1904) is by local man Albert Lambert and much grander, culminating in a

baroque clock-tower. A lofty booking hall extends halfway behind the cab-stand but the platforms make do with low-level roofs fabricated from steel sections; trainsheds and cast iron had gone out of favour.

Another compact plan concentrates all buildings, often with integral canopy, on an island platform with access from a bridge or subway, so the street entrance might simply be a hole in the wall. This was the norm for the last Victorian trunk route: the Great Central link from Nottingham to London (1899). An urban station survives in preservation at Loughborough and a good wayside example at Rothley, both Leicestershire. The West Highland line to Fort William (1894) featured a particularly neat design with offices and waiting area drawn under a wood-shingled roof, as at Tyndrum Upper and Rannoch. An unusually elegant urban example is the Caledonian Railway's Maxwell Park,

Maxwell Park has good period timber detail, notably the awning brackets. Dumbarton Central (1896) is another fine Scottish example of the island platform station; its brick buildings feature stained-glass panels of a mildly Art Nouveau nature.

Glasgow (1894), a wooden building integrated into a glazed verandah, with an upper storey rising in the middle to receive the entrance footbridge.

The Victorians liked towers, and the Great Northern had a brief flirtation with these on its line from Peterborough to Lincoln (John Taylor, 1848). Stocky Italianate campaniles, as at Tattershall, give the railway a distinct style and prominence in this flat landscape, while Lincoln was given a mildly Gothic one. Towers could also help stations stand out amidst the increasing scale of urban buildings. This led the North Eastern to remodel Scarborough's frontage with a slightly absurd baroque edifice in 1883, going on to a more considered design for their new Darlington station

Wemyss Bay station seen from the Isle of Bute ferry.

(1887). These are tall but Eastbourne, East Sussex (1886), demonstrates that height is not always essential, and its little turret, corbelled out from the building, is still an effective foil to the booking hall's prominent lantern roof, a characteristic 'Brighton company' (LBSC) feature. The seed was probably sown by the modest towers tucked into Charles Driver's Gothic designs for the company at Leatherhead and Boxhill, Surrey (1867). In contrast, the Mersey Railway's Hamilton Square station, Birkenhead (1886), has a 37-metre monster but it met a practical need by providing a head of water for the hydraulic lifts to the tunnel platforms far below.

Another clock-tower distinguishes Wemyss Bay, Renfrewshire (1903), the station that took the Caledonian Railway into the twentieth century. The station is a triumph of railway architecture and marks one of the most successful partnerships between engineer and architect, in this case the Caley's Donald Matheson and James Miller, who had worked for the company before entering private practice. It is both railway terminus and ferry terminal, integrated by a concourse sweeping round in a tight curve from the platforms into a covered way leading down to the ships. At its heart is a freestanding, D-plan booking office from which the roof ribs spring out like the spokes of a glass umbrella (title page). The structure is very sturdy but the steel trusses are given arching soffits and made to look comparatively light, while the continued use of traditional cast-iron columns for the platform roofs gives us the best of two visual worlds. Waiting and refreshment rooms wrap round the concourse and are treated externally in the manner of an exclusive golf club of the time, with restrained use of half-timbered gables, climaxing in the tower. The spatial excitement is replicated to some extent in the 1912 reconstruction of Stirling station, which has a similar booking hall and platform roofs, though masked by a stone frontage that seeks to evoke the one it replaced.

GLASS AND THE GREAT TRAINSHEDS

G REAT TRAINSHEDS, WHICH remain the hallmark of railway architecture, first appeared at the start of the 1850s. Dobson's triple-arched shed curving along the tracks at Newcastle (1850) conjured up new vistas, taken up by Brunel at Paddington (1854) on a larger scale. Newcastle's apparent simplicity involves some subterfuge, with the elegantly slender supporting arcades being assisted by a timber truss concealed in the panelling above, whereas Paddington has the full structure on view. Thereafter, multiple-arched spans were favoured by many engineers, even while bold single-span roofs were attracting attention.

Entering Newcastle, one encountered a central concourse, on a scale hitherto unknown, flanked by bay platforms, which handled most of the traffic. One through platform lay ahead, with carriage sidings beyond occupying almost half the shed; space was soon exploited for more platforms, thereby deferring an enlargement of the trainshed until the 1890s.

Paddington had the familiar terminal layout of a dedicated departure platform and offices along one side with an arrival platform on the other. Brunel provided two further island platforms, with carriage sidings between, but pedestrian access was complicated by his extending the tracks into a service area backing on to the hotel, which provides the only formal street frontage. This area eventually became the present concourse. Dramatic vistas are provided by the pair

St Pancras trainshed, with the basement beer store transformed into a shopping area and reception facilities for Channel Tunnel trains.

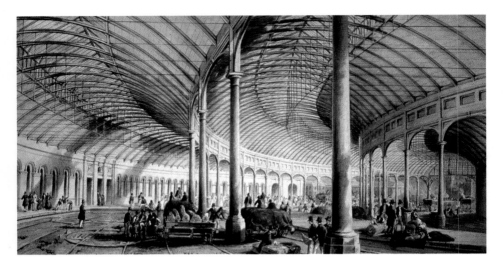

Newcastle Central: interior view by John Dobson with figures by J. W. Carmichael. Note the low platforms (just 0.4 metres high), which were typical of most stations at this time.

of transepts crossing the shed and planned to accommodate carriage traversers, like the one seen at Bristol.

The path to the great single-span roofs was mapped out by the ironfounder Richard Turner, who designed and built a shallow 47-metre arch for a remodelled Liverpool Lime Street. Conceived after Newcastle, it was completed months earlier and pioneered a 'crescent truss', with slender ribs braced by a series of struts and tie rods. The idea was taken up for Birmingham's new central station (1854) but greatly refined by the engineer, Edward Cowper, to provide a more robust roof for a span reaching 65 metres. Consequently, when Lime Street required enlargement again, in 1867, Turner's roof was replaced by the present one, close in scale and concept to Birmingham. The Liverpool shed soon vanished from street view behind a lofty hotel (Alfred Waterhouse, 1871), but emerged again when duplicated by another span in 1879. This remains, but Birmingham New Street lost its roof in 1946.

Lattice girders provide a deeper and stronger beam for the same weight of iron than a solid one, a property exploited by John Fowler for the eastern half of London's Victoria station (1862). Widely spaced lattice arches are braced by lattice

Paddington departure platform: print by Francis Hall after W. P. Frith. The original painting (1862) is the vehicle for a series of cameos but accurately portrays the trainshed and conveys the popular perception of rail travel at the time.

purlins, running lengthwise, and the complexity of Cowper's truss is replaced by a simple array of tie rods. The same scheme was adopted on a larger scale for Glasgow's Queen Street station (1880) but by then St Pancras had transformed people's expectations.

St Pancras station (1868) was a prestige project for the Derby-based Midland Railway. It had extended its main line to London, so that the lucrative coal traffic to the capital would no longer share other companies' crowded tracks, and the new station had to herald its arrival. The line came

Liverpool Lime Street: 1867 span (William Baker). Though based on Cowper's Birmingham roof, the trusses are a lot sturdier and lattice girders are used for the purlins, which run lengthwise and bear the glazing, whereas Cowper had employed wooden beams.

London's Victoria comprised two disparate but adjoining buildings serving different railways. This is Fowler's roof over the 'Chatham' side, which served cross-Channel trains such as the 'Golden Arrow'.

in above street level, so company engineer William Barlow devised a shed with a single span of 75 metres, tied below the tracks, the space underneath being organised as a store for the Burton beer traffic. The trainshed is lofty as well as broad, and very sturdy, with a sequence of closely spaced lattice arches; light streams in through a broad band of ridge-and-furrow glazing. In front stands the hotel, a commission won in competition by Sir George Gilbert Scott, the most popular exponent of the Gothic Revival. Some years elapsed before work began on the hotel, the bulk of which opened in 1873, but the outcome is magnificent.

St Pancras set new standards in terminal planning. For instance, the departure cab road climbed up from a side street into a glazed cab-stand adjoining the booking hall, then emerged through an arch in the hotel frontage. A second arch served an arrival cab road running the full length of the platforms; both are spanned by glazed bridges bearing the hotel's main corridor and betraying Scott's enthusiasm for exposed ironwork. In 2007 the station became the terminal for cross-Channel traffic, and the main access has moved down to the street, the western arch becoming the hotel entrance.

Barlow's trainshed inspired stations in Germany and the United States along with three at home: Manchester Central (1880), Glasgow St Enoch (1876, with second span 1904), and Middlesbrough. St Enoch, as an ensemble, bore the closest resemblance to St Pancras, though Thomas Willson's lofty hotel lacked Scott's panache. The station closed in 1966 and was demolished a decade later. Manchester fared better: it had no frontage building, so the trainshed was readily adapted as an exhibition centre following closure in 1969. Middlesbrough (William Peachey, 1877) remains in

Rarely does a station's rear attract more prominence than its front, but London's Cannon Street (1866) faced over the Thames, so the trainshed was framed by towers, which are the only notable features to survive rebuilding after war damage.

St Pancras, with the former cab exit beneath the tower. The original hotel entrance was through a porch, further left, opening directly off the Euston Road; its splendid interior now houses a stylish public bar.

use but lost its trainshed through war damage. This was much smaller in span (only 23 metres) but very tall and perched high above the street behind a vigorous Gothic office range, which makes a striking impression.

Barlow chose a single-span roof, for practical and economic reasons, but some engineers still favoured multiple smaller roofs. The LNWR, having pioneered large spans at Liverpool and Birmingham, stuck with modest Euston trusses elsewhere. Crewe has a whole cluster but a very handsome late example is Preston (1880), which has lively decorative ironwork accompanying a dignified platform office range. A more stylish approach was the North Eastern's policy of multiple arched spans, initiated by its engineer Thomas Elliot Harrison and beginning with York (1877), which is a richly detailed High Victorian reinterpretation of Newcastle, incorporating ideas from Paddington. Structurally it harks back rather than forward, but the rippling effect of the four spans, building up in scale towards the main one, shows great flair. In contrast to

A nineteenth-century view of York station's interior showing the short carriages then employed.

other railways, the company architect did the detailed design of the trainshed: Thomas Prosser at York, and William Bell at the impressive sequence that followed. Darlington (1887) was the most notable and Hull (1904) the last; by then other roof forms were in fashion.

Arched roofs lift the spirit but a practical alternative was to raise high the glazed ridge-and-furrow roofs already employed on individual platforms. The way forward was shown by two schemes involving the Caledonian Railway and their consulting engineers Blyth and Cunningham: Glasgow Central (1879) and Carlisle (1881). Glasgow Central occupied a site freshly carved from the city centre and the design was probably chosen to maximise natural lighting, taking the form of a fully glazed roof running across a series of impressively deep horizontal trusses. At Carlisle, they had to greatly enlarge a busy station without interrupting traffic, so the trainshed was devised in two spans, with roof bays running along the supporting trusses instead of

Bournemouth (William Jacomb). Approached on foot, the trainshed reads as a great box with tall, vigorously articulated walls, against which the offices keep a respectfully low profile.

crossing them. The ironwork is much lighter than at Glasgow but the spans are significantly shorter. The tracks entered beneath distinctive glazed Gothic screens but these were lost when the roof was reduced in 1954.

The LSWR (London & South Western) followed the Glasgow precedent in their Bournemouth station (1885), though with ornamental features added and the trusses clasped between tall, panelled brick walls that form an uncompromising exterior; simultaneously they added a comparable roof (demolished 1990) to London's Waterloo.

The Forth Bridge (Sir John Fowler and Sir Benjamin Baker). Its contractor, Sir William Arrol, had built the Carlisle trainshed shortly before starting this.

Most designers, however, opted for the Carlisle arrangement, as in the trainshed added to Stoke-on-Trent (1893); there the trusses are external, so all one sees from inside is a rippling glass roof. By then steel had superseded both wrought and cast iron; advances in manufacturing made it cheaper, while the Forth Bridge, completed in 1890, had firmly established its structural credentials. The consequences are seen in the major enlargement of Glasgow Central, completed in 1905 under the direction of the Caledonian's engineer, Donald Matheson. He adapted part of the first

trainshed as a spacious concourse equipped with timber buildings rounded to ease the flow of rush-hour pedestrians, while his extensions virtually tripled the covered area. Steel was exploited to give a much lighter structure than the original, given grace by the gently curved soffits of the trusses. Would that equal flair had been shown in rebuilding the other two big stations with comparable roofs: Edinburgh Waverley (completed 1900) and Waterloo (begun in 1905).

Waverley is remarkable for its centralised plan, with cab roads serving an office range from which most trains could then be reached without crossing the tracks. Looming above is the former railway hotel, entertaining in an elephantine way, but evidence that railway buildings often failed to match the spirit of the great sheds. Indeed, in the 1880s world leadership in large-station design passed to Germany, where state funding helped secure the building of central stations on a lavish scale, notably Frankfurt (1883–8). At the same time the Great Eastern was building its new Norwich station, with a stylish frontage in Northern Renaissance fashion (1886) but no trainshed, just a short concourse roof and low-level platform awnings; this would become common practice in the twentieth century.

Glasgow Central: view through the 1905 extension from the suburban platforms over the cab road towards the main-line platforms.

NEW IDEAS: 1900–39

BY 1900 MOST companies saw little need for further route mileage, and focused on improvements. The largest station scheme was Waterloo, a product of haphazard growth, where all but the recent (1885) section was gradually replaced by a spacious, well-planned but visually unexciting ensemble. Working round the traffic made it a slow job, further delayed by the First World War; completion came in 1922 with the dedication of the 'Victory Arch', the LSWR war-memorial entrance.

In 1905 the North Eastern completed its reconstruction of Hull, with the last multi-span arched trainshed to be built in Britain, though these continued to emerge in Germany. The Great Western rebuilt Birmingham Snow Hill (1912, demolished) with a ridge-and-furrow roof but echoed the previous arched shed in a glazed cab-stand cum booking hall. The trainshed was superseded entirely at Aberdeen (1914), its place taken by a spacious concourse hall accompanied by individual platform roofs in the manner of recent Caledonian work at Perth (1911). This planning reflected American practice, as did the pared-back classicism of the frontage, making it in some ways the most progressive British station of its generation.

Aberdeen was a co-operative venture by two companies, whereas the façade of London's Victoria embodies Edwardian grandiloquence and company rivalry. On the right we see the 'Brighton' line's tall 'Frenchy' frontage, which accompanied a total rebuilding of its station in 1908. On the left is the 'Chatham' company's aggressively baroque response. This, however, met a civic need as their station was London's gateway for foreign dignitaries arriving on the boat trains from Dover, where an imposing Marine station, in aptly Beaux Arts manner, was completed in 1915.

Some of this period's smaller stations were lessons in stylish dignity. Barkingside, in east London (1903), is a very refined essay responding to the proximity of Barnardo's 'Village Home' for orphan girls. Upmarket commuters were the LNWR target when they called in Gerald Horsley to design some north London examples, notably Hatch End (1911) – a richly detailed 'Wrenaissance' pavilion with hipped roof and cupola. Whitley Bay, Tyne and Wear, was both commuter town and seaside resort, so a dash of Jacobean flavour was stirred into its station (1911), whose lofty clock-tower was a lodestone for day trippers.

London's Underground had begun with shallow, steam-operated routes, most stations having arched roofs slung over a cutting, as at Notting Hill Gate (1868), though Baker Street (1863) demonstrates the alternative – a brick vault built directly under the road, with slanting shafts for ventilation and natural lighting. The deep electric 'tube' lines (1890 onwards) required only small surface booking halls, often over-built and needing a distinctive house style to make them conspicuous. From 1906 this was provided by Leslie Green's steel-framed buildings with façades in 'ox-blood' red faience, Chalk Farm (1907) being a good example.

Aberdeen, around 1975, looking from concourse to platforms. The departure indicator, left, employed a youth walking behind the windows to place individual numbers and destination blinds by hand.

Barkingside. Other stations on the Great Eastern's 1903 line from Woodford to Ilford employ a standard design by their architect, W. N. Ashbee, but this is an outside commission, though with typical GER platform roofs.

The First World War forced the railways into co-operation, which Parliament afterwards consolidated by legislating to merge them into three new companies – the London Midland & Scottish (LMS), London & North Eastern (LNER) and the Southern (SR) – plus an enlarged Great Western (GWR), a grouping effective from 1923. They soon faced falling revenues from key industries, notably coal and steel, accompanied by a loss of rural traffic to a rising competitor, road motor transport. Thus there was limited investment in buildings outside three programmes: Southern electrification, Great Western renewal, and London Underground expansion.

The Underground's consulting architect, Charles Holden, developed designs of a distinct modern character, often for surface stations on network extensions. Lofty booking halls, such as Arnos Grove, betray Continental influence and give the system a bold, distinct identity that attracted international attention. Southgate (1933) exemplifies integration, with its island ticket hall, partly encircled by bus stances and a shopping parade. Hall and platform roofs employ reinforced concrete and range from slab roofs and bow-ended waiting rooms at Sudbury Town

(1931) to the stylish trainshed at Cockfosters (1933). The meticulous detailing throughout is tribute to Holden's Arts and Crafts background.

Among main-line architects, the Southern's John Scott found himself busiest. Rationalisation in Kent brought new stations at Ramsgate and Margate (1926), their vaulted halls hinting at pre-war American Beaux Arts designs. These carry more visual conviction than the weak Wrenaissance that followed at, for example, Exeter Central (1933). This was not the image to accompany electrification, so 1938 brought a rash of contemporary designs. Bishopstone, East Sussex, is one of several featuring prominent booking halls derived from Holden but lacking his flair. South-west London acquired Odeon-style essays at Richmond and Surbiton, the latter's finned tower embracing an unusual double-decker footbridge – parcels above passengers. Horsham, West Sussex, is the most intriguing. The curving frontage seems rather quirky until you realise that the shallow concrete awning and the prominent wrap-over window above the entrance are derived from a widely published modernist exemplar – the much larger Florence station (1936).

Arnos Grove (Charles Holden, 1932). The interior retains its 'passimeter', a combined booth for ticket purchase and inspection, as a display feature. This is a surface station, and the platforms have concrete roofs along with original furnishings.

Ramsgate was probably designed by Maxwell Fry, later a noted modernist, during his few years with Scott. The large windows express the station hall whereas Exeter Central, for example, could be mistaken for a contemporary post-office.

Surbiton and Horsham make extensive use of reinforced concrete but the platform roofs remained steel-framed. However, the Chessington branch stations in south-west London (1938) introduced arching concrete canopies. Chessington North is particularly striking, with concrete

Only twenty-seven years separate Surbiton (left) and Whitley Bay (right). William Bell's Whitley Bay tower is just for show whereas the Surbiton ones housed parcels lifts serving the upper level of the bridge.

walls clasping the railway embankment, rising up into the station and flowing along into a road bridge.

Largest of the grouped companies was the LMS, stretching from Dorset to the Pentland Firth. Inheriting a generally sound building stock, it avoided much new construction but saw value in a modern image. The LMS first embraced modernity with Morecambe's stylish Midland Hotel (1933). A small hotel by railway standards, it was intended to lure wealthy travellers, so they went outside the company to Oliver Hill, who provided just what was needed – a gently British interpretation of Continental modernism, featuring sleek curves and bold horizontal lines.

Ignoring the pompous clumsiness of Euston House (1934), the next attempt at modernist credentials, we come to Leeds City (1938), the showpiece large station scheme. Platforms and roofing remained largely as they were, having outgrown the modest trainshed, but this made way for a new hotel and concourse. The latter, designed by company architect William Hamlyn, was the focus. Instead of the obvious glazed steel hall, Hamlyn opted for a succession of lattice steel portal frames, plastered over and implying concrete. Along with a

Horsham. The parcels office and footbridge have a feature entrance off to the left, from which a broad corridor curves round the station front to the booking hall and main entrance.

Midland Hotel, Morecambe. Oliver Hill was permitted to commission work from prominent artists, notably the sculptor Eric Gill, whose relief of Neptune and Triton looks down on the main staircase.

deep, coffered ceiling, it evoked a weighty modernity and brought space, light and order to a hitherto cluttered and dingy station (see contents page). Curtis Green was consultant for the hotel, and his modernised neo-Greek touches inside are entertaining, but the façade is dour. It fronts the city's main square, where nothing too modern was welcome, so it reads as an austere stone cliff with classical features tacked on near the top. Rebuilding Euston station was to follow but, despite its being formally inaugurated in 1938, nothing had happened before war broke out.

The LMS adopted reinforced concrete for some smallish stations, typified by Apsley, Hertfordshire, and Hoylake, Wirral (both 1938). The offices have a concrete frame, with brick infill panels, bearing a cast slab roof cantilevered out and canted up to form a platform canopy, its neat, slender edge made possible by heavy beams lying out of sight above. Apsley is the basic version, whereas Hoylake is larger and has the canopy swooping round to shelter a taxi rank. Girvan, Ayrshire (1951), is a deferred LMS scheme that draws on some of these features.

The Great Western carried out far more rebuilding schemes than the LMS, including Newton Abbot (1925), Swansea

Hoylake: sketch by its architect, William Henry Hamlyn, highlighting the canopy wrapped round a totem pole and the circular clerestory of the booking hall.

(1932), Cardiff (1934) and Leamington Spa (1938), and the enlargement of Aberystwyth (1924), Newport (1930), Taunton (1932), Paddington (1934) and Bristol (1935). Some were unavoidable replacements for 'Brunel barns' whose lives could be prolonged no further; all were spacious and well-planned, but flair was a variable factor and GWR architect Percy Culverhouse seemed to teeter awkwardly between modernity and tradition.

Bristol: the new platforms of 1935 feature almost identical buildings to Cardiff, faced in Carrara-ware faience with moulded lettering in GWR chocolate.

Cardiff seeks to be a showpiece. We enter below rail level through a large hall that outwardly respects the Portland-stone neo-classical idiom established at Cathays Park, the city's institutional heart. Yet the interior is not radically different from Hamlyn's later Leeds essay, apart from the weak detailing. The platform buildings make a good but ambivalent show: hints of Tudor in the mullioned windows, and hints of Art Deco above. Platform roofs revert from the riveted stanchions of Edwardian times to cast-iron columns, with attractive results not unlike late Caledonian designs. Stylistic uncertainty surfaces also at Leamington, outwardly a

modernised-Georgian response to the town's stucco terraces, but the platforms mingle Art Deco windows and doors among traditional ones.

The LNER was hardest hit by the economic situation and had to focus investment on improving freight facilities while basing its public image on new streamlined express trains; fortunately, it inherited a good, sound building stock. Tradition typified early stations such as Berwick-upon-Tweed (1927), based on a pre-war scheme and featuring handsome bow-windowed timber platform buildings. Clacton (1929) is stolidly neo-Georgian, but Doncaster's huge entrance hall (1938) has minimal detail and good proportions. Main-line widening north of York (1933) featured country stations in a thoughtful modernised-Georgian; of these only Otterington survives. Art Deco featured in several new booking offices but Modernist essays were few. One stands apart: Loughton, Essex (1940), where J. M. Easton produced a stark brick-box booking hall and stylish concrete canopies.

Otterington station and signalbox: a carefully detailed essay in modernised-Georgian manner by Robert Darling of the LNER York office. The small-windowed ends housed a lock-up store and toilets, the centre an office and waiting room.

CHANGING NEEDS: 1939–2013

THE SECOND WORLD War, when the railways were working flat out and much routine maintenance was necessarily postponed, was followed by nationalisation in 1948. State investment was meagre compared with that on the Continent and in buildings priority was given to engine sheds and freight facilities.

The first new station of quality was Potters Bar, Hertfordshire (1955), with slender, pre-stressed concrete platform roofs, since rebuilt. Banbury, Oxfordshire (1959), pioneered a layout that made the footbridge the station core, sandwiching waiting rooms and toilets between segregated parcels and passenger corridors. More stylish versions followed at Harlow, Essex, and Broxbourne, Hertfordshire.

Harlow (1960), serving the new town designated in 1947, features bands of glazing capped by flat roofs with deep overhanging fascias – particularly striking where they cascade down over the platform steps. Broxbourne is more grittily impressive, reading as a gault-brick box shooting over the tracks, then dropping down to earth to form the booking hall.

The much larger Coventry station (1962) responded to a rebuilt city centre and new cathedral with a sleek glass box – the entrance hall, continuing at one end as the bridge, while its roof flies out at the other as a portal. The layout, though, is conventional, with all facilities at platform level. Route electrification funded Coventry and the remarkable Manchester Oxford Road (1960), where nested timber shells roof a tapering concourse. These are borne by laminated timber arches, echoed in the platform roofs.

Electrification revived interest in quickly assembled modular buildings for wayside stations. An LMS prototype with light steel frame and enamelled iron cladding panels (1945) had been followed by a production model at Marsh Lane, Liverpool (1947, demolished), but work then stalled for a decade. The new design was more complex than the LMS one and expensive, so, after use on lines from Crewe to Manchester and Liverpool, it was dropped. Hartford, Cheshire (1961), illustrates the visual havoc wrought by later alterations when fashions had changed and the original components were no longer available.

It was cheaper to adopt a system already in production, so the Southern Region tested out the CLASP school-building scheme at Guildford signalbox (1966), and then stayed with it for a decade. Most applications were offices and relay rooms but about thirty stations were rebuilt as well. A typical example, incorporating platform awnings, is Strood, Kent, which replaced a timber building. Despite its progressive image, with concrete panels hung on a steel frame, features such as timber window frames required regular maintenance,

Broxbourne (Peter Reyniers, 1960). Through the entrance-hall window we see the robust concrete bridge deck. A vertical accent, emphasised by contrasting brick, is provided by the lift towers, originally intended for parcels movement.

Manchester Oxford Road (Max Clendinning and Hugh Tottenham). Concealed steel reinforcement (1998) has been used to cure the onset of structural weakness.

so thoughtful rearrangement of substantial Victorian buildings would generally have served better.

By the late 1960s the traditional concept of a wayside station was becoming obsolete. Staff were costly and on many routes 'pay trains', with onboard ticket sales, were the only economic option. Unstaffed buildings became vulnerable and many were replaced by simple platform shelters.

Seeking money for capital investment, British Rail increasingly turned to commercial development of major sites. Many were abandoned freight facilities, but the 'air rights' over stations were potentially lucrative. Birmingham New Street (1967) was the first big scheme, and an unmitigated disaster, bequeathing inadequate access to narrow platforms under a low slab. By the 1980s confidence was reviving and the railway was something to celebrate, so at Charing Cross the hotel and concourse remained while the undistinguished trainshed (1905) was replaced by an office block (Terry Farrell, 1991), whose arched forms recall the original 1864 roof. Enough headroom was left beneath to create a pleasant platform environment.

The major achievement of this time is Liverpool Street, whose trainshed (Edward Wilson, 1875) is a unique design, with lofty columns bearing two main spans intersected by a sequence of narrower aisle roofs, the filigree work in these

Liverpool Street: the 1991 concourse and roof. The platforms are below street level, where a mezzanine gallery serves a line of shops, in modern glass tunnel idiom, which define the concourse edge without compromising the vistas through the trainshed.

contrasting with the bold simplicity of the main trusses. An 1894 extension had left the station in three distinct sections without satisfactory links. Office development above these later platforms and on the site of neighbouring Broad Street station funded an imaginative remodelling (Nick Derbyshire, 1991) that extended the trainshed to cover a large new concourse.

Trainsheds are back in fashion, though we have nothing yet to match Santiago Calatrava's sculptural lyricism at Liège-Guillemins. London's Docklands Railway produced César Pelli's stylish glass shed elevated between office towers at Canary Wharf (1987), while the Channel Tunnel justified a more prominent essay at Waterloo (Nicholas Grimshaw, 1993). Continental traffic moved in 2007 to a remodelled St Pancras (Alastair Lansley), occupying the Barlow shed and part of a huge but low-key northward extension, which is shared with domestic services. The main entrance has moved to the interface between these, while, in a brilliant stroke, a slot cut through Barlow's trainshed floor created a shopping and Eurostar concourse with remarkable vistas.

Neighbouring King's Cross (Lewis Cubitt, 1852) posed a problem. It followed the Lime Street plan of offices down one side of the trainshed and a screen front. Economy was

demanded, so the shed roofs were borne originally on laminated timber arches, echoed in the huge windows of the boldly simple façade. The interior served largely as a carriage shed but was gradually filled with platforms, requiring a linking concourse, for which there was no room. The railway heads straight into tunnels, so the shed could not be lengthened, while there was little space in front and no desire to mask Cubitt's façade. Temporary buildings served until a new concourse, with a showpiece roof, was wrapped round the original office range (John McAslan, 2012).

Burgeoning passenger traffic rendered several 1960s schemes inadequate within thirty years. Leeds has been remodelled (2002) with a high-level roof replacing the paltry industrial shed of 1966, while Birmingham New Street's new west concourse (2013) is the first step in a major improvement. Also in 2013, a large hall was completed over the tracks at the rebuilt Reading station, while work progressed on the total renewal of London Bridge, London's oldest terminal site. Meanwhile, improvements in technology have enabled Network Rail to revisit the modular concept, beginning with stations at Mitcham Eastfields, south London (2007), and Corby, Northamptonshire (2008).

King's Cross concourse roof gushes up in front of Cubitt's stark booking office. His abilities show up better in the great screen front, at last freed of the clutter that had already begun to obscure it in the nineteenth century.

THE LARGER PICTURE

Passenger stations are the railway's public face but many other buildings were formerly essential to its operation. Until the 1960s a typical country town would have had a goods station, coal yard and cattle dock, a water tower and probably an engine shed. Most stations had a signalbox, generally controlling an array of mechanical semaphore signals and points; some had several. Out in the country there were lineside platelayers' huts for men maintaining the track, and these were the subject of a successful modular design.

The four grouped companies each had concrete workshops, manufacturing precast components for structures such as platforms. The Southern was particularly well known for concrete footbridges, seats, lamp-posts and 'fencing' but it also developed concrete lineside huts, with their roofs profiled to fit on a flat wagon for delivery by rail. The LNER developed a modular alternative for assembly on site, and this continued in use well after nationalisation.

Though already found at major stations and junctions, signalboxes did not become common until the 1870s. The basic concept is a glazed operating floor set high enough to give a good view, with (originally) mechanical safety interlocking housed in a room below. Shrewsbury's Severn Bridge Junction (1903) is a standard LNWR design raised very high, and by 2013 the largest mechanical box remaining in Europe. Site restrictions could require a box spanning the railway but only a few 'bridge boxes' survived into the twenty-first century,

Haltwhistle, Northumberland. Built in 1861 to the design of Newcastle & Carlisle Railway's final engineer, Peter Tate.

such as Canterbury West (1928) and Wylam, Northumberland (1897).

Most railways had their individual designs, though the differences were often superficial, such as the steep roofs and frilly bargeboards characterising the Great Northern. The grouped companies continued to differ. Some of the most modern-looking LNER buildings were the control towers that accompanied new goods sorting yards, but these did not enter its brand image, whereas the Southern quickly became identified with the Moderne signalbox design introduced at Surbiton in 1936.

After nationalisation regional forms persisted, but Hackney Downs (1960) typifies good practice, with its deep overhanging roof fascia to minimise solar glare. Britain never got the costly showpiece buildings seen at Zurich, for example, but Birmingham New Street (1967) and Liverpool

Wayside concrete. A gatekeeper's cabin built with the LNER system of concrete panels slotted into upright posts, and a Southern platelayers' hut.

New overtrack signalboxes on the approach to London Bridge station, 1866. Letters on the semaphore arms indicate the movements they controlled.

Dorking (Surrey) signalbox dates from 1938 and is a good example of the Southern's Moderne style. Where these boxes were sited between running lines the operating floor was bow-ended, with windows wrapping right round, as at Wimbledon.

Street (1991) are very distinctive. Since technology now allows one signalling centre to control routes any distance away, signalbox numbers are steadily declining. In 1900 there were around thirteen thousand; by 1994 this had fallen to about one thousand. In 2012 Network Rail operated around five hundred and forecast an ultimate reduction to just fourteen centres. This will still leave some conserved *in situ* and adapted for other purposes, such as Totnes, Devon, a 1923 example of traditional GWR design, or York (1877), both now cafés. Others continue to serve their original purpose on preserved railways.

The typical goods transhipment shed housed a track running past a wooden platform with docks for road carts to back into, but these had vanished from the operational scene by the early 1970s, with the focus on container and bulk traffic. Goathland, North Yorkshire (1865), displays one in preservation along with discharging cells for coal and lime, while the National Railway Museum is partly housed in a large urban example at York (1877).

Some locations justified multi-storey buildings with storage above one or two transhipment floors, as at Manchester's Great Northern warehouse (1898), now a leisure centre. The LNWR's

A Caledonian Railway signalbox from Coatbridge overlooks LNER no. 246 emerging from the Scottish Railway Preservation Society's Bo'ness station, graced by the 1842 trainshed from Edinburgh's Haymarket station.

canalside warehouse at Chalk Farm in north London is another good example, used as offices and accompanied by extensive horse stables, now housing a market. Horses were immensely important for shunting and cartage, and the railways still had over nine thousand in 1948, but the last went in 1967. In contrast to London's multi-storey stabling, Monkwearmouth, Sunderland, has a more conventional hundred-horse stable (1884) grouped round an enclosed yard and still recognisable despite decades in industrial use.

Acklington goods shed, Northumberland (1847, recorded 1973, now a dwelling). Benjamin Green designed this to match his Jacobethan station, a style maintained in the later stable, whose open door beckons.

FURTHER READING

Addyman, John, and Fawcett, Bill. *The High Level Bridge & Newcastle Central Station.* North Eastern Railway Association, 1999.

Anderson, Roy, and Fox, Gregory. *A Pictorial Record of LMS Architecture.* Oxford Publishing Co., 1981.

Biddle, Gordon. *Britain's Historic Railway Buildings: A Gazetteer.* Ian Allan, 2011.

Biddle, Gordon. *Great Railway Stations of Britain.* David & Charles, 1986.

Bryan, Tim. *Railway Workshops.* Shire, 2012.

Fawcett, Bill. *A History of North Eastern Railway Architecture.* North Eastern Railway Association, 3 vols: 2001, 2003, 2005.

Fitzgerald, Ron. *Liverpool Road Station, Manchester.* Manchester University Press, 1980.

Foster, Richard. *Birmingham New Street.* Wild Swan, 3 vols: 1990, 1997.

Hoare, John. *Sussex Railway Architecture.* Harvester Press, 1979.

Johnston, Colin, and Hume, John. *Glasgow Stations.* David & Charles, 1979.

Lawrence, David. *Bright Underground Spaces: the railway stations of Charles Holden.* Capital Transport, 2008.

Minnis, John. *Southern Country Stations: South Eastern & Chatham Railway.* Ian Allan, 1985.

Moore, Andrew. *Leicestershire's Stations.* Laurel House, 1998.

Oakley, Mike. *Devon Railway Stations.* Dovecote Press, 2007.

Signalling Study Group. *The Signal Box.* Oxford Publishing Co., 1986.

Simmons, Jack, and Thorne, Robert. *St Pancras Station.* Historical Publications, 2003.

Vaughan, Adrian. *A Pictorial Record of Great Western Architecture.* Oxford Publishing Co., 1977.

INDEX